DESIGNS IN SCIENCE
USING SOUND

SALLY and ADRIAN MORGAN

Using Sound
Copyright © 1994 by Evans Brothers Limited

Facts On File, Inc.
460 Park Avenue South
New York NY 10016

Library of Congress Cataloging-in-Publication Data
Morgan, Sally.
    Using sound / Sally and Adrian Morgan.
        p. cm. — (Designs in science)
    Includes index.
    ISBN 0-8160-2981-4
    1. Sound — Juvenile literature. 2. Sound-waves — Juvenile literature. [1. Sound.] I. Morgan, Adrian. II. Title.
III. Series: Morgan, Sally.   Designs in science.
QC225.5.M67   1994
534—dc20   93-31720

Facts On File books are available at special discounts when purchased in bulk quantities for businesses, associations, institutions or sales promotions. Please call our Special Sales Department in New York at 212/683-2244 or 800/322-8755.

10 9 8 7 6 5 4 3 2 1

This book is printed on acid-free paper.

Printed by Wing King Tong

Editor: Su Swallow
Designer: Neil Sayer
Production: Peter Thompson
Illustrations: Hardlines, Charlbury
                David McAllister

Acknowledgments

The authors and publishers would like to thank Andrew Hingley for valuable help on chapter 6, Recording and reproducing sound.

For permission to reproduce copyright material the authors and publishers gratefully acknowledge the following:

Cover Michael Fogden, Bruce Coleman Limited
Title page Michel Tcherevkoff, The Image Bank
Contents page Sally Morgan, Ecoscene
Page 6 (top) Johnny Johnson, Bruce Coleman Ltd, (middle) The Image Bank **page 7** Richard Megna, Fundamental, Science Photo Library **page 9** (top) Robert Harding Picture Library, (middle) Warren Faidley, Oxford Scientific Films **page 10** (left) Andrea Pistolesi, The Image Bank, (right) Ian Harwood, Ecoscene **page 11** Peter Terry, Bruce Coleman Ltd **page 12** (top) Sally Morgan, Ecoscene, (bottom) Topham Picture Source **page 13** (middle) Sally Morgan, Ecoscene, (bottom) Ford Motor Company **page 14** Jonathan Scott, Planet Earth Pictures **page 15** Jane Burton, Bruce Coleman Limited **page 16** (top) Jonathan Scott, Planet Earth Pictures, (bottom) Philip Craven, Robert Harding Picture Library **page 17** J.A.L. Cooke, Oxford Scientific Films **page 18** (top) Robert Erwin, Natural History Photographic Agency, (middle) Chris Priest, Science Photo Library **page 19** Lorenzo Lees, Ecoscene **page 20** (middle) Professor C Ferlaud, CNRI, Science Photo Library, (bottom) David Redfern, Redferns **page 21** (top) Michael Fogden, Oxford Scientific Films, (middle) J Cancalosi, Bruce Coleman Limited **page 22** (top) William M Smithey Jr, Planet Earth Pictures, (middle) Uwe Walz, Bruce Coleman Ltd **page 23** Altan Power, Bruce Coleman Ltd **page 24** (top) James D Watt, Oxford Scientific Films, (middle) Jay Freis, The Image Bank **page 25** (top) Odile Noel, Redferns, (bottom left) The Hutchison Library, (bottom right) Richard Megna, Science Photo Library **page 27** (top) Sally Morgan, Ecoscene, (bottom) Queen Productions Ltd **page 28** (top) Richie Aaron, Redferns, (bottom) Towse, Ecoscene **page 29** Chris Huxley, Planet Earth Pictures **page 30** The Image Bank **page 31** (top) J.A.L. Cooke, Oxford Scientific Films, (middle) Michael Holford, (bottom) Sally Morgan, Ecoscene **page 32** Roger Miller, The Image Bank **page 33** Sally Morgan, Ecoscene **page 34** Andy Purcell, Bruce Coleman Ltd **page 35** (main) Robert Francis, Robert Harding Picture Library, (inset) Ray Ellis, Science Photo Library **page 36** (top) Robert Harding Picture Library, (bottom) Dr Tony Brain, Science Photo Library **page 37** Sony United Kingdom Limited **page 38** Luiz Claudio Marigo, Bruce Coleman Ltd **page 39** (top) Kim Taylor, Bruce Coleman Ltd, (middle) Dennis Green, Bruce Coleman Ltd **page 40** Marcus Morgan **page 41** (top) Marcus Morgan, (middle) Philip Chapman, Planet Earth Pictures **page 42** (left) Larry Mulvehill, Science Photo Library, (right) Alan Towse, Ecoscene **page 43** (top) Frank Whitney, The Image Bank, (bottom) Masud Qureshi, Bruce Coleman Ltd **page 44** Robert Harding Picture Library **page 45** (top) Adam Woolfitt, Robert Harding Picture Library, (bottom) Martyn F Chillmaid, Robert Harding Picture Library

USING SOUND

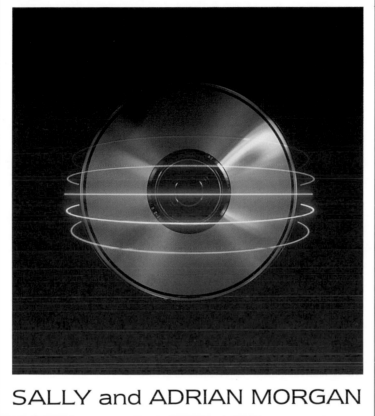

SALLY and ADRIAN MORGAN

Facts On File

NOTE ON MEASUREMENTS:

In this book, we have provided U.S. equivalents for metric measurements when appropriate for readers who are more familiar with these units. However, as most scientific formulas are calculated in metric units, metric units are given first and are used alone in formulas.

Measurement

These abbreviations are used in this book.

METRIC		**U.S. EQUIVALENT**	
Units of length			
km	kilometer	mi.	mile
m	meter	yd.	yard
cm	centimeter	ft.	foot
mm	millimeter	in. or "	inch
Units of speed			
km/h	kilometers per hour	mph	miles per hour
km/s	kilometers per second	mi./sec.	miles per second
Units of time			
h	hour	h	hour
s	second	s	second
ms	millisecond	ms	millisecond
Units of frequency			
Hz	Hertz	Hz	Hertz
Units of temperature			
°C	degrees Celsius	°F	degrees Fahrenheit
Units of loudness			
dB	decible	dB	decibel

Using Sound is one book in the Designs in Science series. The series is designed to develop young people's knowledge and understanding of the basic principles of movement, structures, energy, light, sound, materials, and water, using an integrated science approach. A central theme running through the series is the close link between design in the natural world and design in modern technology.

Contents

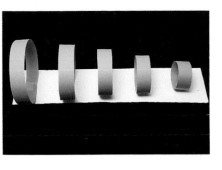

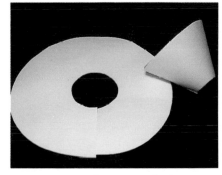

Introduction

Both people (right) and other animals, such as these elephant seals (above), use sound as a means of communication.

Sound is such a familiar part of our lives that we tend to take it for granted. However, it is extremely useful to us. We rely on sound for communication through forms of speech and music. Unexpected noises often warn us of danger. Even faint background noise can tell us a great deal about our surroundings.

The animal kingdom also uses sound to communicate. Many animals make particular sounds to warn of danger or to attract a mate. Bats and dolphins navigate by using sound. One species of shrimp even employs sound as a weapon to stun its prey.

We think of the world as a very noisy place, but human beings can hear only a small proportion of the sounds made by other animals. Many of the sounds that animals emit are outside the range of our hearing. In the same way, not all animals are able to hear all the sounds that humans can. Each animal has its own range of hearing adapted to its environment and to its way of life.

What is a sound?

A sound wave is a series of differences in pressure, as first the air is compressed and then expands again. It is similar to the way waves of tight coils move along this spring.

Sounds are made when an object vibrates. For example, when a drumstick hits the surface of a drum, the flexible skin of the drum vibrates up and down, moving the air immediately above it. When the skin moves up, the air is squashed together (compressed) and the air pressure becomes higher than normal. When the skin moves down, the air expands and the air pressure becomes lower

Sound can be shown as a waveform on the screen of an oscilloscope. The sound waves are converted into electrical signals that are displayed as a series of waves on the screen.

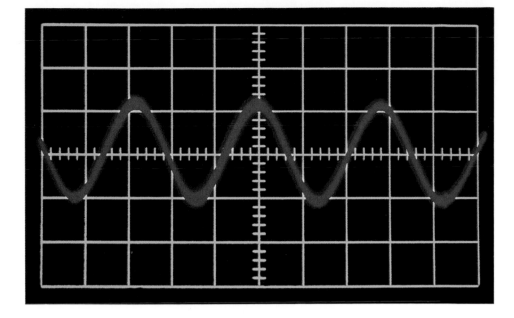

than normal. The pressure differences in the air travel away from the surface of the drum, like ripples in a pond. This effect produces a sound wave.

Sound is a form of energy. Sound waves transfer sound energy from one place to another, but they need particles of matter, such as atoms and molecules, to pass the energy onward. The sound waves cause these particles to vibrate so that they bump into one another and transfer sound energy. This means that sound is able to move through air, liquids and solids. However, sound cannot travel through a vacuum because a vacuum contains no particles. Space is a vacuum, so there are no sounds in space.

The speed at which a sound wave travels away from the source is called the speed of sound. It depends on the substance through which the sound is moving (and the temperature). For example, it is 340 m/s (1,130 ft./sec.) in air and 1500 m/s (4,950 ft./sec.) in water (at room temperature of 18°C or 64.4°F). It can travel faster through liquids as there are more particles to vibrate. Sound travels even faster through solids.

It is not possible to see sound, but it can be shown by an instrument called an oscilloscope. A microphone (see page 17) picks up the sound waves and turns their vibrations into electrical signals. The electrical signals are picked up by the oscilloscope, which displays the signals as a series of waves on a screen. The sound waveforms can then be measured and recorded.

This book examines the role of sound in the lives of animals, including humans, and how animals make and hear sounds. It describes the way sound can be produced by human-made objects and shows how we are able to talk to somebody on the other side of the world.

Important words are explained at the end of each section under the heading of **Key words** and in the glossary on page 46. You will find some amazing facts in each section, together with some experiments and some questions for you to think about.

Key words
Vibration a back and forth movement, or oscillation.
Wave a disturbance in a medium such as air or water, occurring at regular intervals.

Sound waves

The movement of waves across the surface of water is produced by the up and down motion of particles in the water. They are called transverse waves. Sound waves, on the other hand, are longitudinal: they are caused by a back and forth movement of particles.

If you throw a stone into a pond or lake, a ring of small waves appears on the surface of the water. The waves spread out in ever increasing circles from the place where the stone entered the water. The larger the stone, the larger are the waves. Sound waves moving away from a sound source form a very similar pattern to the ripples formed on the surface of water.

There are a number of technical terms that are connected to sound waves. *Wavelength* means the distance between the crest or trough of consecutive waves (waves that follow one after another). The height of the wave is called its *amplitude*. Sound waves with a greater amplitude will sound louder. This is because they carry more sound energy.

The speed of the sound waves is measured by counting the number of waves that pass a particular spot in one second. This is known as the *frequency*. It is usually recorded as the number of waves per second. The greater the number of waves per second, the greater the frequency. Small objects can vibrate more rapidly than large objects and so produce sounds of a higher frequency. High frequency sounds have a high pitch or note, while low frequency sounds have a lower pitch. Frequency is measured in Hertz (abbreviated as Hz), which is simply a measure of the number of sound waves per second. For example, 200 Hz indicates a sound that produces 200 sound waves per second.

Low and high frequency waves may sound different, but they all move at the same speed. For example, in air a high frequency sound of 200 Hz and a low frequency sound of 20 Hz will both travel at 340 m/s. This means that for the high frequency sound ten times as many sound waves will pass a particular point in one second as for the low frequency sound.

The speed of sound depends on the material through which the sound is traveling (see page 7). Sound travels faster in liquids than in air because the particles in the liquid are more numerous and packed closer together. This means that the sound energy can be passed on more quickly. Solids contain many particles densely packed together. This means that sound waves can pass even more quickly through solids than either liquids or air. For example the speed of sound through glass is 5000 m/s (16,500 ft./sec.).

The speed of sound in air (340m/s) has a special name - Mach 1. Twice the speed of sound is known as Mach 2, and so on.

Wavelengths of different sounds

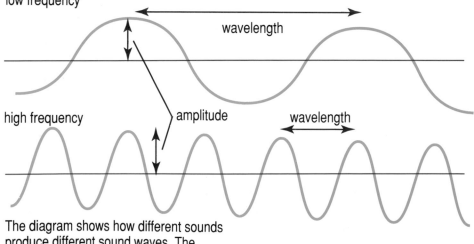

The diagram shows how different sounds produce different sound waves. The sounds are of the same loudness, so the amplitude is the same height, but one sound has a higher frequency than the other.

What is the difference between sound waves and waves moving across water?

A sonic boom can be produced naturally during a thunderstorm (below) and by machines such as the Concorde aircraft (right).

Why do you see a flash of lightning before you hear thunder?

If you stood near a jet engine, you would experience sounds of about 150 dB – enough to damage your hearing. A particularly quiet sound, like that of rustling leaves, may be as low as 10 dB.

Supersonic aircraft, such as the Concorde, can travel at speeds greater than the speed of sound. This creates a "sonic boom" or shock wave that follows the path of the aircraft. The sonic boom is powerful enough to break glass. A clap of thunder is an example of a natural sonic boom. In a thunderstorm, lightning produces a huge electrical spark that travels between the thunder clouds and the ground at very high speed. As the spark passes through the air it heats it, causing the air to expand. As soon as the spark has passed, the air contracts, moving faster than the speed of sound. This extremely fast movement of the air produces a sonic boom. It is possible to estimate how far away a thunderstorm is by timing the interval between observing the lightning and hearing the boom. Sound takes approximately three seconds to travel one kilometer, so by counting the seconds between the lightning flash and the accompanying clap of thunder, and then dividing this number by three, it is possible to work out the distance of the storm.

The loudness of a sound depends on the energy within the sound wave itself. In general, the greater the height of the peaks of a sound wave (its amplitude), the louder is the sound. The loudness of a sound is measured in decibels (dB). Zero dB is a sound level just below that which can be heard by humans and 125 dB is the point at which sound becomes painful to the human ear. The decibels scale is not linear, but logarithmic. This means that the amplitude of a 2 dB sound is 10 times that of a sound of 1 dB, not twice the amplitude.

The Doppler effect

You may have noticed that, as an ambulance or police car approaches with its siren sounding, the note of the sound gets higher in pitch. As the vehicle goes past and starts to move away from you, the sounds get lower. This is known as the Doppler effect, after the Austrian scientist who first described it. The change in pitch occurs because the source of the sound is moving in relation to the position of the listener. If the sound source is moving toward the listener, the interval between each successive wave is reduced, so it appears to have a higher frequency. Conversely, if the source and listener are moving apart, the waves reach the listener less frequently. The sound then appears to have a lower frequency, so the pitch also becomes lower.

Sound reflection

Sounds do not travel very far in air. The particles in air are spaced far apart and they do not bump into each other as frequently as particles moving in a liquid do. The pressure wave creating the sound quickly spreads out in all directions and the sound rapidly becomes fainter. Sound travels better over water, because the surface of the water reflects the sound waves back into the air. This is very similar to the way light is reflected off a mirror. For this reason, voices may sound very loud in a swimming pool. It also explains why it is often possible to hear sounds quite clearly from across a lake. Sounds can also be reflected off walls too. The Whispering Gallery of St. Paul's Cathedral in London shows how effective this can be. The sounds are almost perfectly reflected by the walls of the dome, with the result that quiet whispers made on one side of the gallery can be clearly heard on the other side. Many

The Whispering Gallery of St. Paul's Cathedral in London gets its name because whispers on one side can be heard clearly on the other.

The sounds made by these children (right) reflect off the surface of the water, so the sounds appear to be much louder.

concert halls and other large public auditoriums are specially designed to enable everybody in the audience to hear well, even those sitting at the back. The science of the generation and control of sound is called acoustics (see page 32).

The distance that a sound wave can travel also varies. For example, low frequency sounds travel further than those with high frequencies. This is because of the length of the sound wave. The wavelength of a particular sound can be found by dividing the speed at which it is traveling by its frequency. Sound in air travels at 340 m/s. Therefore a sound with a frequency of 20 Hz (i.e., 20 sound waves per second) would have a wavelength of 17m (340 divided by 20). Such long sound waves contain a lot of energy and can easily travel around objects in their path. Sounds with higher frequencies have much shorter wavelengths. These shorter sound waves are less energetic and more easily obstructed. They tend to bounce off, or to be absorbed by, even relatively small objects. It is for these reasons that the parts of music you can hear being played in a neighboring room tend to be the lower frequencies, such as the bass. It is also the reason why fog horns give out low frequency sounds that can be heard over many miles. Sirens, by contrast, are always high frequency sounds that can be heard above the noise of the traffic.

Ancient Greek theaters, such as this one in Epidaurus, were built more than 2,000 years ago. They have excellent acoustics. An actor speaking softly or a coin dropped on the stage can be heard quite clearly from the back rows, even though the theater is in the open air.

Resonance

When objects vibrate, they do so most easily at one particular frequency. If an object is allowed to vibrate freely, it will do so at its own natural frequency. This frequency depends upon the object's shape, size and material from which the object is constructed. For example, tapping a small bell at its natural frequency produces a ringing note, known as its fundamental note. A larger bell, made of exactly the same material and of identical shape, will have a lower natural frequency, and so will produce a lower frequency fundamental note.

Resonance occurs when energy is given to an object at the same rate as its natural frequency. It can be likened to pushing somebody on a swing. In order to get the swing to move well, the pusher has to time each push carefully. If he or she does not push

! *Human beings have a fundamental frequency. People have felt sick in some buildings in which the air in the ventilation system was pulsing at the same rate as the natural frequency of the human stomach (approximately 3Hz).*

These Indonesian instruments will resonate at one particular frequency.

Some professional singers can produce a note so perfect in pitch that they can cause a glass to pick up enough energy to shatter.

Why do you think soldiers are asked to march out of step when crossing bridges?

at the right time, a good oscillation (swing) will not be produced. The pusher will end up reducing the swing. He or she has to match the frequency of the pushes to the frequency of the moving swing.

Resonance can be a surprisingly powerful effect. It is very important in playing musical instruments. If a musician plays a note that has the same fundamental frequency as a glass on a table nearby, the glass will start to vibrate as it picks up sound energy from the surrounding vibrating air. Resonance will occur if the instrument is vibrating at exactly the same frequency causing the air around the glass to vibrate at the natural frequency of the glass.

Most structures tend to resonate at one or more frequencies (that is, they have more than one natural frequency). Resonance can cause spectacular damage if it occurs where it is not allowed for. Engineers have to consider this effect when building modern bridges. Often the bridge is built with a special aerodynamic shape to prevent energy from moving currents of air from setting up resonance in the bridge deck. The effect of this resonance might otherwise cause the bridge to sway and possibly even to collapse.

In an earthquake, the frequency with which the earth moves up and down may be the same as the natural frequency of a particular building. The energy from the vibration set up by the earthquake may cause the building to collapse. Engineers have to ensure that the new structures in earthquake zones have a natural frequency well outside the range of any natural vibration that

On November 7, 1940 the Tacoma Narrows Bridge over Puget Sound in Washington collapsed as a result of vibrations set up by gusting winds. The vibrations matched the natural resonance of the bridge and, by giving additional energy to the structure, caused its eventual collapse.

Resonating rings

To discover how objects of different sizes vibrate at different frequencies, all you will need is a piece of cardboard 30–40 cm (12–16 in.) long and 10 cm (4 in.) wide, a large sheet of thick paper, tape and a pair of scissors.

1 Cut five strips of paper, each approximately 3 cm (1 in.) wide. Cut the strips to the following lengths: 46, 40, 34, 28 and 22 cm (18, 16, 14, 12 and 10 in.).

2 Bend the strips into rings and tape the ends of each strip together to keep it in position.

3 Place the rings along the cardboard at an equal distance from one another. Secure each ring in place with a single piece of tape.

4 Now shake the cardboard backward and forward, slowly at first but gradually increasing in frequency. Watch the rings. They should all start to vibrate, but each ring will resonate (vibrate most strongly) at a different frequency. You should find that the largest ring starts to resonate first and the smallest will resonate last, at a higher frequency.

5 If you continue to shake the cardboard even faster, you should notice that the largest ring begins to resonate again, but at a much higher frequency. This is because each ring will resonate at more than one frequency. However, the shape of the vibrating ring will depend on the frequency. For example, the ring may have a round shape when it resonates at one particular frequency, but be squarer when it resonates at another.

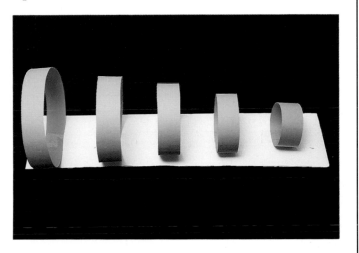

could occur. Resonance has also to be damped in moving objects such as cars. This is particularly important in eliminating unwanted sounds. Vibrations, created by the wheels moving over the ground and the moving of the engine parts, often cause significant noise. To overcome the problem of noise, car manufacturers add shock absorbers to the wheels, make engine mountings from rubber to reduce the vibrations transmitted to the body shell and add foam padding to the body work.

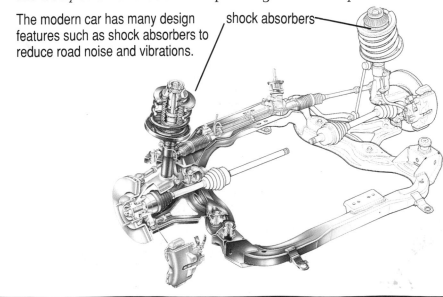

The modern car has many design features such as shock absorbers to reduce road noise and vibrations. — shock absorbers

Key words
Amplitude the height of the peak of a wave above an imaginary line running along the middle of the wave form.
Frequency the number of sound waves that pass a particular point per second.
Pitch a measure of the frequency of a sound, for example a high frequency sound has a high pitch.
Resonance a condition that occurs when an object is vibrated at a frequency matching one of its own natural vibrations.

Collecting sound waves

Sound waves do not carry a lot of sound energy and they do not spread very far in air. Over millions of years, therefore, many animals have developed special organs to help them detect and amplify weak sound waves. They then turn them into signals that can be passed to the brain. The ear is one of the results of this process of evolution. People have also developed electronic equipment that can pick up, amplify and transmit sound waves. Such inventions enable us to communicate quickly and clearly over long distances.

Ears

The ears of this deer are large and they can be rotated to help pinpoint the source of a sound.

The ears of mammals have evolved into highly specialized structures that collect and amplify sound waves before passing them on to the brain. Such ears all have a similar structure, although there are certain adaptations to suit the lifestyle of each particular mammal.

An ear consists of three parts: the outer, middle and inner ear. The outer ear is the part we can see on the outside of the head. Its scientific name is the pinna. The pinna's function is to collect the sound waves and funnel them into the middle ear. The shape of the pinna varies between different species of mammal. For example, rabbits and deer have very large outer ears. These collect sound waves very efficiently and so give the mammal acute (sharp) hearing. Some mammals can also control the direction in which the pinna points, thereby reducing the effects of unwanted noise from other directions and allowing the mammal to determine the source of a noise more accurately.

The middle ear is encased in bone for protection. The outer and middle ear are separated by a membrane called the ear drum or tympanum. Within the middle ear are three tiny ear bones, the hammer (the smallest in the body), the anvil and the stirrup. They are collectively called the ossicles. These bones are carefully positioned and held in place by muscles. When sound waves arrive at the ear drum from the pinna, they cause the ear drum to vibrate. As the eardrum vibrates, it moves the hammer. This in turn pushes on the anvil, causing the anvil to vibrate. Finally the vibrations reach the stirrup. Together, the ossicles cause the

The Human Ear

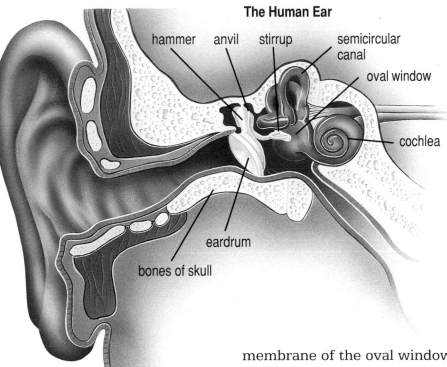

hammer anvil stirrup semicircular canal

oval window

cochlea

eardrum

bones of skull

vibrations to be amplified by about 22 times. There is no loss of sound as the vibrations are passed from bone to bone. The vibrating stirrup touches a membrane called the oval window, which forms the boundary between the middle and inner ear.

The inner ear is different from the middle and outer ear in that it is filled with fluid rather than air. It contains two organs: one for hearing and one for balance. The hearing part of the inner ear is the cochlea, which is a coiled, fluid-filled structure containing receptors. These receptors are connected to nerves. When the membrane of the oval window starts to vibrate, it pushes on the fluid in the cochlea, which also begins to vibrate. The fluid in the cochlea pushes on the receptors, causing messages to be sent along the auditory nerve to the brain.

The second type of structure in the inner ear are the semicircular canals. These are highly specialized sensors that provide the brain with information concerning the position and movement of the head. There are three semicircular canals, lying at right angles to each other, enabling the brain to detect movement in all directions. When the head is moved from side to side, fluid in one of the semicircular canals starts to move. The moving fluid pushes on sensory hairs located within the semicircular canal. The hairs send information to the brain, providing information on the position of the head. This information is used by the brain to control balance and posture.

Some mammals have ears that are specially adapted to give them better hearing. The fennec fox is a desert dweller that hunts mainly at night when it is cooler, so it needs acute hearing to detect its prey. Its large ears are particularly efficient at collecting sound. They also help the fox to keep cool during the heat of the day, as the fox's blood flows very close to the surface of the ear's skin. This allows heat energy to be transferred to the surrounding air quite readily, mostly by radiation.

The kangaroo rat also lives in the desert. It is preyed upon by snakes and owls, both of which have excellent senses to help them hunt. The eardrum of the kangaroo rat is very large, as is its middle ear. However, the oval window

The large ears of the fennec fox give the animal excellent hearing.

Some nocturnal moths have a very wide hearing range that extends from 1,000 Hz to an astonishing 240,000 Hz.

The hippo (right) has very small ears. Can you think of any reasons why this is so?

between the middle and inner ear is particularly small. There is therefore a considerable difference in size between the eardrum and the oval window that enables the kangaroo rat to magnify low frequency sounds by as much as 100 times. The hearing of the kangaroo rat is so sensitive that it can hear the sound of air flowing over the wing of an owl or the scales of a snake moving across the sand, giving it advance warning of a predator's approach.

Human ears are located on either side of the head. They are not very good at collecting sound waves but are ideally positioned for locating sounds. Sound waves will arrive at one ear first, then the other. For example, a sound coming from the right of our head will arrive at the right ear a few thousandths of a second before it arrives at the left. By comparing the signals from each ear, the brain can work out the approximate direction of the sound source. We tend to turn one ear toward the direction of the sound to maximize the difference in the time of arrival in one ear and the other of the sound. This helps our brains locate the source of the sound more precisely.

Barn owls can work out the direction and height of a sound, which is particularly useful when they are hunting. The barn owl's peculiar ability to do this is created by the characteristic ruff of feathers on its face. The ruff is formed by two rows of tightly packed feathers that funnel sound waves toward the ears. One of the owl's ears is positioned slightly higher than the other. The channel in the feathers on the right tilts up to collect sound waves from above, while the

The barn owl hunts at night and so relies on acute hearing to find its prey.

channel in the feathers on the left tilts down and emphasizes sound from below. By comparing signals from each ear, the owl is able to distinguish the height as well as the direction of the sound. The owl also devotes a large proportion of its brain to building a "sound map" of an area, allowing it to locate and memorize sounds without needing to move its head.

Hearing range

The ability of animals to hear sounds varies. In general, larger animals hear and use low frequency sounds, while small animals hear and use high frequencies. For example, mice have a hearing range of 1,000 to 100,000 Hz, while a cat has a range of 30 to 45,000 Hz and an elephant has a range of 20 to 10,000 Hz. However, there are some exceptions to this general rule. The

A spadefoot toad

spadefoot toad lives in desert habitats, and it spends the dry season buried in the ground. It only emerges after the infrequent rains form pools. Its young have to develop in these pools before the water dries up. The spadefoot toad's hearing is designed to be very sensitive to the low frequency sounds of rain falling on the ground, so that it knows when to emerge and spawn.

Insects hear sounds too, but they have very different types of ears. An insect ear consists simply of a membrane with some receptor cells. Certain insects have clumps of specialized hairs, while others have specially adapted antennae to collect sounds.

Microphones

In scientific terms, microphones are described as energy transducers. This means that they change sound energy into electrical energy. This relies upon an effect known as induction. An electric current is induced in a piece of wire if it is moved in and out of a magnetic field. The more quickly the wire is moved, the greater the current that is produced.

A microphone contains a thin membrane called a diaphragm, usually made of plastic, metal or mica (a thin layer of a crystal). The diaphragm is connected to a tube that has a wire coiled around it. The sound waves cause the diaphragm to vibrate which, in turn, causes the tube to move in and out. The tube is held in a magnetic field and the movement of the tube causes movement or kinetic energy to be transformed into electrical energy. The electrical current created in the coil is carried along connecting wires to the amplifier and from there to the loudspeaker.

A loudspeaker works rather like a microphone in reverse. However, the flow of an electric current along wire held in a magnetic field causes electrical energy to be transformed into kinetic energy. The electric current is passed through a coil that is wound around a tube. The tube is attached to a paper cone that is held in a magnetic field. Electrical energy passing through a coil within a magnetic field is transformed into

A microphone

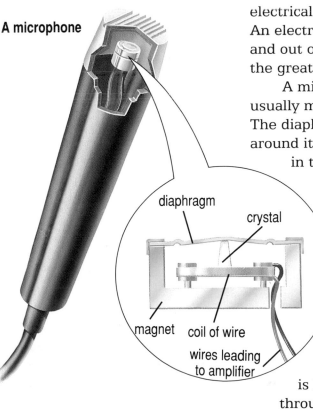

diaphragm

crystal

magnet   coil of wire

wires leading to amplifier

Both the ear of a kangaroo rat (right) and a hearing aid (below) magnify the sound waves. The latest hearing aids are so small that they can fit into the ear or be hidden in the frame of a pair of glasses.

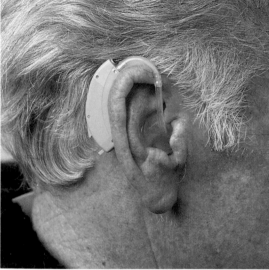

kinetic energy and this causes the coil to move, and hence moves the paper cone in and out. The movements of the cone set up pressure waves in the air, heard as sound. The sound is louder because the amplifier has strengthened the signal coming from the microphone. A stronger signal will cause the paper cone to move further.

Deafness is a condition in which a person or animal is unable to hear sounds. For example, the sound waves may not be able to reach the cochlea in the inner ear, or the cochlea may be unable to send signals to the brain. If it is not possible to solve the problem with medical or surgical treatment, a person suffering such a problem may be given a hearing aid. This device consists of a small microphone, which detects the sound waves, linked to an amplifier. The amplifier magnifies sound waves (rather like the ear of the kangaroo rat, see page 15), passing them on to a tiny loudspeaker that directs the sound waves into the ear. The hearing aid is usually powered by a small battery.

Telephones

Telephones make use of a small microphone and loudspeaker. The basic technology of the telephone has remained much the same since it was invented by Alexander Graham Bell in 1876. Early telephones relied on the principle that carbon granules change their electrical resistance under pressure. This means that when the carbon granules are pushed together, an electric current can pass through more easily. In a telephone, the carbon granules were held in place by two carbon blocks. The front, dome-shaped block was attached to a flexible diaphragm and could move

A telephone
The earpiece contains an electromagnet

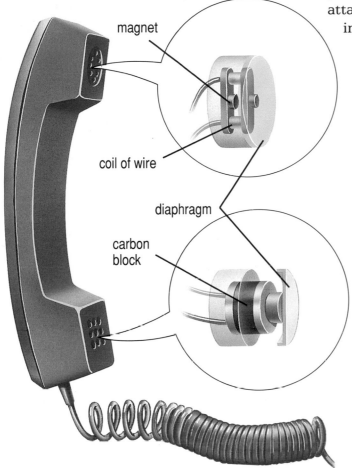

magnet

coil of wire

diaphragm

carbon block

backward and forward. The rear, cup-shaped block was fixed firmly in position and could not move. Both blocks were attached to an electricity supply. When someone spoke into the mouthpiece, the changing air pressure caused the diaphragm to vibrate. The vibrations were passed on to the carbon granules. The pressure on the carbon granules varied continuously. A louder sound would cause the granules to be pushed together more than a quiet sound. This reduced the electrical resistance, allowing more current to flow through them. A loud sound, therefore, would produce a larger electrical current. The changing current was a direct copy of the changes in the air pressure created by the voice. Modern telephones use the same basic techniques, but they are much smaller, lighter and more efficient.

The earpiece of a telephone converts electrical energy into sound in a similar way to that described for a loudspeaker (see page 17). The electrical current is passed along wires wrapped around a magnet. The magnet is located close to a diaphragm. The changes in the current in the wire affect the pull of the magnet on the diaphragm, which moves in and out with the changing current. This creates vibrations that form sound waves, which travel through the air.

A modern telephone

Key words
Ear an organ concerned with hearing in animals.
Loudspeaker an electromechanical device that converts electrical signals into sound waves.
Microphone a device that converts sound waves into electrical signals.

Making sounds

Many animals use sound to communicate with one another, and the ways in which animals make sounds are basically the same. Humans have now learned how to make artificial sounds as well, by using a vast array of instruments and machines. Nevertheless, the way the sound is produced is very similar to the methods employed in the natural world.

Animal communication

The human voice is produced by the larynx – a hollow, box-like structure in the windpipe. It can be seen and felt as a lump on the front of the neck, often called the "Adam's Apple" or "voice box". The larynx contains bands of fibers that vibrate as air passes across them. The vibrations produce sounds. If you touch your larynx and speak, you will feel it vibrating. One end of each vocal cord is attached to the front wall of the larynx, while the other end is attached to one of two movable cartilages within the larynx itself. When you inhale, the vocal cords are pulled apart and air passes through on its way to the lungs. As you exhale without speaking, the vocal cords remain apart. However, in order to sing or speak, the two cartilages are moved closer together as the air is breathed out. This partly blocks the windpipe, so the air has to push past the cords, which then start to vibrate. The length and thickness of the vocal cords, together with the size of the larynx, all contribute to the pitch of the voice. A male human has a deeper voice than a female because he has a larger larynx with longer and thicker cords. Fine control of the vocal cords allows us to produce a wide variety of sounds. When a child learns to speak, the child is as much learning how to control his or her vocal cords to make the desired sound as he or she is learning to use a language.

The vocal cords in this photograph are stretched across the windpipe, leaving just a triangular hole for the air to pass through.

Young boys have a small larynx and they can produce high pitched notes. When boys reach puberty, their voices "break" and become lower in pitch.

Animals can communicate in many different ways, including the use of visual signals and scent, but sound is the method most commonly used for long-distance communication or where visibility is restricted such as in dense jungle.

Most nocturnal (night-time) animals rely heavily on sound for communication. Among the noisiest groups of nocturnal animals are the frogs. In North America, during the bullfrog breeding season, ponds and marshes can be deafeningly noisy places in the early evening. Although the noise seems very confusing to our

? *Why do some birds in rainforests produce low frequency sounds rather than high frequency ones?*

The sounds made by this toad are amplified by the inflated air sac.

ears, most frogs are only sensitive to a narrow band of frequencies – the one that their species uses to call. So each call, and the frequency at which it is made, is characteristic of an individual species of frog. The sound is often amplified (see page 30) by a large sac of air at the frog's throat. The air sac acts in the same way as the body of an acoustic guitar (see page 27). The air inside resonates, and hence acts as a natural amplifier of the frog's croak. Insects create sounds in a different way. The cicada vibrates the membranes on its abdomen very fast. Grass-hoppers rub their notched thighs against the edge of their wing to make a sound.

! *The rattlesnake warns other animals that it is dangerous by shaking the rattle at the end of its tail.*

The rattlesnake (right) is so named because of the rattle sound made by the end of its tail.

Bird sounds

? *Why do woodpeckers drum their low frequency messages on dead tree trunks rather than on healthy living trees?*

Birds are probably the group of animals best known for their ability to make sounds. While mammals produce sounds in their larynx, and use their lips and tongues to project and modify the sound, birds have a different voice organ, called the syrinx. The syrinx is located near the lungs and consists of a resonating chamber and a number of membranes. Air from the bird's lungs is driven through the syrinx as it breathes out. The membranes are then tightened, relaxed and moved in relation to the resonating

As swans fly (right), they produce an almost musical sound, known as flight music. The sound is created by the beating wing feathers. Some scientists think that these sounds may help swans to keep the flock together.

The yellowhammer may repeat its song as often as 1,000 times each day.

The famous too-whit-too-whoo call of the tawny owl is really the sound of two birds. The first owl sings too-whit and the second replies too-whoo.

chamber to produce each different sound. Muscles around the syrinx can also change the shape of the syrinx, further altering the sounds produced. Smaller birds produce more high frequency sounds. For example, the tiny wren produces high frequency sounds at around 4,000 Hz. It sings 56 notes in just 5.2 seconds, creating a very rapidly changing song. The wren's song can be properly heard by humans only if it is recorded and then played back again slowly.

Birds use their songs primarily to identify their territory, to give warning calls and to attract a mate. Most bird species that sing can be identified quite easily by their song. Birds with drab plumage tend to sing more loudly than those that have colorful feathers, since they must rely on their voices to attract attention. Many bird songs are repeated several times over to make sure the message gets through. The yellowhammer, for example, repeats its song as often as 1,000 times each day. The onset of daylight is a key factor affecting bird song and, for the 20–40 minutes around dawn, more birds sing than at any other time of day. This is known as the dawn chorus, and it is particularly noisy in the spring during the breeding season.

Immersed in sound

! *Dolphins can make more than 30 different sounds. The meaning of each can be modified by the dolphin changing its posture, for example by nodding its head, at the same time as it makes the sound.*

Sounds are particularly important for animals that live in water. They cannot use many of the senses that terrestrial animals would use, for example sight and smell. In the oceans there is little light and smells do not spread out far from their source. However, water is an ideal medium for sound, as sound travels five times faster through water than through air. The sound waves travel over much greater distances and at the surface of the water they are reflected back down into the depths. For a long time scientists thought that oceans were silent places. They were very wrong. A wide range of animals make sounds, including crustaceans, fish and the marine mammals. Even the sound of surf crashing onto a rocky beach travels far out into the oceans.

Recently many residents of San Francisco's harbor have experienced the power of animal communication. People living in houseboats moored along the coastline of San Francisco Bay complained of being kept awake at night by a persistent loud

This insignificant-looking toadfish produces a loud humming sound by vibrating its air bladder.

humming. Many theories were put forward regarding the source, until it was eventually tracked down to a small fish. The toadfish had started to colonize the harbor, following a clean-up program to reduce the pollution there. During the spawning season, the male toadfish were "singing" to attract females. They made a humming sound by vibrating their air bladders. This singing would continue for about an hour. The toadfish swam in the sea near the houseboats, and the hollow hulls of the houseboats acted as amplifiers for the sounds. The people of San Francisco harbor could not get rid of the fish, so now, during the spawning season, they hold an annual Toadfish Festival.

Whales are remarkable communicators and can remain in touch over vast distances. They do not produce clicks as dolphins do. Instead, the males sing. The "song" of the humpback whale consists of roars, groans, squawks and chirps. A single song is about 10–20 minutes long, but the singing can last for several hours or even days. Humpback whales from different parts of the world have different songs. As a group of whales travels the oceans, some bits are added to the song and others removed; so that the songs gradually change over time. Humpback whales come together for about three months to mate. At the start of the mating season the whales sing the song with which they ended the previous mating season. The song gradually changes during the mating season.

The blue whale, the largest living animal in the world, has a song of particularly deep moans. It has a large larynx and huge lungs, so it can produce very low, loud notes. These loud sounds

The song of the humpback whale is a complex mix of groans, grunts, chirps and squawks repeated over and over again.

Many military ships make use of the sound channels in the oceans.

are very powerful, reaching more than 180 dB. The blue whale's song can echo across oceans from coast to coast.

Many whales, including the fin whale and the blue whale, make use of a specific channel in the ocean through which sound travels very well. These factors change with depth. At 1,500 m (4,950 ft.) below the surface of the ocean there is a special "layer" of water created by the temperature, salinity (saltiness) and pressure of the water. The combination causes this particular layer to act as a kind of channel, confining sounds within it. Sound waves bounce off the top and bottom of the channel, just as if the top and bottom were solid. For this reason, sound can travel through this channel for thousands of miles without significant weakening. Whales take advantage of this channel to send messages to other whales on the far side of the ocean.

The navies of many countries also make use of these sound channels in the sea. The channels are used for a process called *so*und *f*ixing *a*nd *r*anging (known as sofar) because sounds travel so well in this channel. For example, naval vessels can track submarines. Unfortunately this means that the whale songs now have to compete with all the human-made sounds in this special channel, as well as with all the sounds nearer the surface produced by modern shipping fleets.

Musical instruments

What is the difference between a musical sound and noise?

Musical notes, like all sounds, are produced by pressure waves from vibrating objects. Musical instruments can be made of pieces of wood, metal, string and even tubes containing a vibrating column of air. Notes of musical instruments are based on octaves. Each time the pitch of a sound goes up by one octave, the frequency of that sound has doubled. Most instruments also require some means of amplifying the sounds they make. For example, a single violin string does not make much of a sound when it is plucked, but if the string is stretched across a hollow box, the sound is much louder as both the box and the air within it vibrate in time with the string. This resonance amplifies the sound.

Large musical instruments produce low notes in the same way that large animals produce low, loud sounds. For example, a young child can sing much higher notes than an adult. There is a similar progression from a viola to a violin to a cello. A wind instrument, such as a flute, has a number of holes along the length of the tube. As the instrument is played, certain of the holes are covered up and uncovered. This alters the frequency at which the instrument resonates, thereby changing the notes.

Resonance can occur when the frequency of the vibrations is also a fraction or a multiple of the natural frequency. The notes produced by these resonant frequencies are higher than the note played and are called harmonics.

The body of the violin amplifies the sounds produced when the string is plucked.

A wind instrument relies on air resonating within the tube.

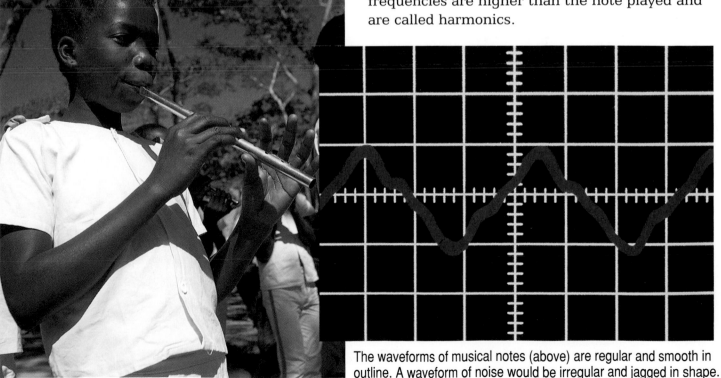

The waveforms of musical notes (above) are regular and smooth in outline. A waveform of noise would be irregular and jagged in shape.

Stringed instruments

Can you name two instruments in which sound is produced by plucking the strings, another two in which sound is produced by hitting the strings and two more which are bowed?

! *Some of the most perfect violins in the world were made by Antonio Stradivarius during the late 17th and early 18th centuries. Modern technology has been unable to reproduce the quality of acoustics he created by hand!*

Sounds are produced on a stringed instrument by plucking, hitting or bowing the string. A guitar player, for example, produces sounds by plucking the strings, using either fingers or a small piece of plastic known as a plectrum (pick). The length of the string is controlled by the player's fingers, which press the string against raised ridges of metal on the fingerboard. These ridges are known as frets. The pitch of a note depends on the length of the string, the tension at which it is held and the thickness of the string. If the tension on a guitar string is increased (that is, pulled tighter), the string will vibrate more rapidly and the note will have a higher pitch. A thick string is used to produce a lower note. Guitar strings are designed so that, when they are at the correct tension, they can play six notes - E, A, D, G, B and the next E.

Each musical note consists of a basic or fundamental note, together with a number of higher sounds, called harmonics. On a guitar, each open string – a string that is not held down – produces a different fundamental, each with its own series of harmonics. The ear hears a combination of these sounds, but the fundamental is the strongest sound. By holding the string down at different points, the player can produce different fundamentals, each of which will have its own series of harmonics (see artwork below). It is the combination of fundamentals and harmonics that gives each type of instrument its own tone (sound quality).

Many rock and pop groups use electric instruments. Most modern groups use two or more electric guitars, each producing a different sound. The lead guitar usually has six strings while the

In this diagram, the bottom line represents the vibration of a string that has been plucked. This is a fundamental. The whole string moves up and down (1). At the same time, other vibrations are taking place along the string: the two halves are moving up and down (2), and other smaller parts are also moving up and down independently (3-8). Each set of vibrations produces a different harmonic, higher in pitch than the fundamental. If the fundamental in this series of harmonics is the note C, then the second, fourth and eighth harmonics will also be a C, each one an octave higher than the one below.

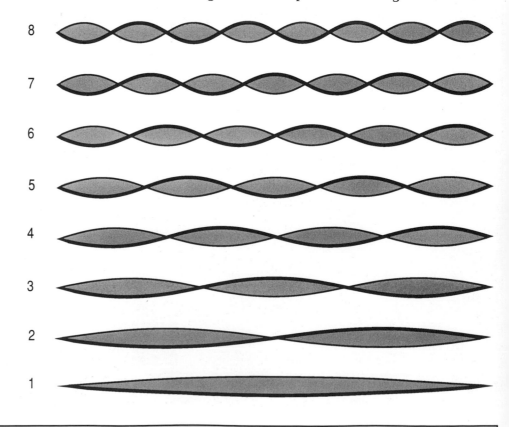

EXPERIMENT

A simple guitar

You can make a very simple guitar with a sound box from household items. You will need two plastic containers without lids, one small and the other larger, and a selection of rubber bands of varying thickness.

1 Stretch the rubber bands around one of the boxes as shown in the photograph.

2 Pluck the bands to discover the sound that they produce. What is the difference in sound produced by a thick band compared to a thinner band?

3 Repeat the experiment using the rubber bands on the other plastic container. What effect does the size of the box have on the sound?

The sound of a modern rock group such as Queen is created by a mixture of vocals, electric guitars, drums and keyboards. Microphones, amplifiers and loudspeakers make the sounds very much louder.

bass guitar has only four. The electric guitar is relatively slim since all the amplification is carried out by electronics. The sound waves are converted to electric signals by small microphones, one beneath each string (see page 17). The electric signals are magnified in an amplifier and are sent to a loudspeaker that reproduces the sound waves.

Wind instruments

The flute has a fixed length of tube. The length of the tube can be changed and different notes produced by depressing certain keys.

Wind instruments work on a different principle than stringed instruments. Air is blown into them, and the column of air trapped within the instrument vibrates. The frequency of the sound this creates is determined by the length of the tube. The longest wind instruments will produce the lowest notes. A short column of air, such as that in the flute, vibrates more quickly than that of a larger instrument like an oboe, so it produces higher notes. The pitch of each note can be altered by changing the effective length of the tube. In the trombone, this is done by sliding a U-shaped piece of tube in and out, thus physically lengthening the air space. However, many wind instruments, for example the recorder or clarinet, have a fixed-length tube. The length of the tube is changed by opening or covering holes in the side, which produces the correct musical notes.

Why do you think you hear the sea when you hold a seashell to your ear?

EXPERIMENT

Panpipes

Panpipes are an ancient form of musical instrument that consists of a series of tubes of different lengths. The air inside the pipes is made to vibrate by blowing into the pipe. The pipes are of different lengths, and so will produce a variety of sounds. You will need 5 tubes (cardboard rolls, mailing tubes, even rubber piping), a piece of stiff cardboard approximately 30 cm (12 in.) long and 10 cm (4 in.) wide, a pair of scissors and tape.

1 Cut the tubes to varying lengths, for example 100 cm (40 in.), 75 cm (30 in.), 50 cm (20 in.), 25 cm (10 in.) and 12 cm (5 in.).

2 Using the tape, stick the tubes to the cardboard in order of length.

3 Before playing the pipes, stand in a room where there is some music playing or people talking. Listen to the sound through each of the pipes in turn. Compare the sounds that you hear in each of the pipes. The sounds in the room will be a mixture of frequencies, but the pipes separate out these frequencies. The

longest pipes will pick up the lowest frequencies, since the column of air in the tube is the longest and the air vibrates more slowly. Is there a difference in frequency if you put your ear right up against the end of the pipe, rather than just close to it?

4 Now try playing the pipes by blowing across the ends. What sounds can you produce?

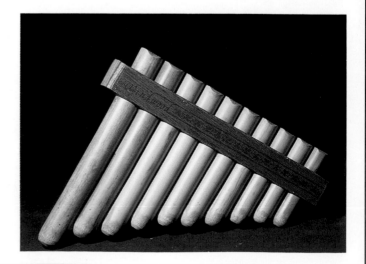

Drums

How does the tension in the skin of a drum affect the note that can be produced?

Drums are one of the oldest of all musical instruments. They are found all over the world and come in all shapes and sizes. Their method of construction is extremely simple. A skin of material is stretched over a hollow container so that, when the skin is hit with the hand or a stick, the skin and the air inside vibrate to produce a drumbeat (see page 6). The tone of the note produced depends on a number of factors, including the size of the drum head. The larger the head, the lower is the note. Tightening the skin of the drum also has an important effect on the note. This is because making the skin tighter will reduce the duration of the sound, as well as raise its tone slightly. The volume of air inside also affects the tone of the note. The more air the drum contains, the lower are the notes produced.

Sonic weapons

These pistol shrimps catch their prey using sonic weapons.

Sound can be dangerous to animals. It can damage ears and even kill. Some animals make use of sound when they hunt their prey. For example, the pistol shrimp uses sound to stun small fish. It has a special claw, kept open by two discs that are held in place by suction. When the claws are closed, the discs are pulled apart, releasing the suction and producing a clicking sound. This click is loud enough to be heard under water over one kilometer away. Any fish within a few inches of the claws is stunned for a moment. While it is still disoriented, the shrimp will seize it and let off a few more clicks to kill it.

Sperm whales also hunt by stunning through sound. They are able to produce powerful bursts of sound within a complex series of nasal passages. The sound is amplified using a special oil-filled organ in their head. When released, the sound energy can be concentrated into a burst of sound that reaches 265 decibels (dB). This burst of sound is large enough to kill squid and small fish. Human ears would start to hurt at 125 dB. Other toothed whales, such as the fin whale, also use stunning sound to disorient shoals of fish, so that the fish are easier to catch. It is difficult to imagine how the sound is produced, but it is a little like taking a deep breath and then letting it out in one go - the air rushes out and the throat emits a sound. It is rather like a sneeze!

Key words
Fundamental the lowest harmonic of a musical tone.
Harmonics a series of partial vibrations that combine to form a musical tone.
Larynx the organ that produces sound in mammals.

Amplification and soundproofing

It is often useful to be able to make a sound louder, so that it is carried further. At other times it is important to be able to reduce the amplitude of a sound. The science that investigates the behaviour of sound is called acoustics.

Making sounds louder

Once a sound has been produced, it spreads out from the source where it was made. Because of the spreading, the sound gets gradually weaker as it travels outward. However, it is possible to direct sound so that it travels more strongly in one direction. For example, if somebody wants to make themselves heard more easily, they can cup their hands around their mouth to concentrate the sound in a particular direction. The sound level is amplified by this concentration. A megaphone is a device that does the same thing as cupped hands, using a horn shape to direct the sound. Modern megaphones also use electronics to increase the power at the source of the sound. Hi-fi loudspeakers are constructed from cones of paper that perform the same function (see page 17).

Amplifiers are used in the natural world too. For example the air sac in the throat of male amphibians such as frogs and toads (see page 21) contains a lot of air that will resonate. This serves to

Cupped hands form a natural megaphone. Directing the sound in this way enables people to communicate over greater distances.

amplify the male frog's call so that it can be heard by female frogs. The male mole cricket makes its call by rubbing its wings, just like grasshoppers. However, to ensure that the sound carries to the female, the male mole cricket builds an amplifier. It burrows down into the soil and excavates a sound chamber at the bottom of the hole. This sound chamber is exactly the right size and shape to resonate at the same frequency as the sounds made by the cricket's wings when they are rubbed. The insect is able to check that the chamber is resonating correctly by detecting changes in the pressure waves produced by the sounds. The sound chamber is very similar in function to the horn amplifiers that were attached to old-fashioned gramophones.

A mole cricket (above right) constructs a sound chamber to amplify its mating call. Human-made horn amplifiers used in old-fashioned gramophones (right) amplify sound in the same way.

EXPERIMENT

Making a megaphone

In this experiment you will discover how to amplify the sound waves of your voice. You will need a large piece of cardboard, scissors, tape and a friend to help you.

1 Cut out a circle of cardboard, 60 cm (2 ft.) in diameter with a central hole of a diameter of 15 cm (6 in.). Make a slit from the outside to the inner circle.

2 Roll the cardboard into a cone shape and secure it in position with tape.

3 Go outside and ask your friend to stand about 10 m (33 ft.) away. Talk in a normal voice to your friend. Can she or he hear you?

4 Say the same thing, but this time talk into the megaphone. Does this make any difference to the loudness of your voice? Does the distance between your friend and yourself seem to make any difference?

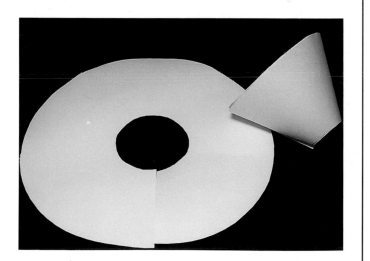

5 Repeat this experiment using a smaller megaphone. Cut down the circle of cardboard, so that it has a diameter of 50 cm (20 in.). How might you improve this experiment? How could you measure the loudness of your voice more accurately?

Acoustics

The quality of sound in a concert hall depends on its acoustics. The way in which the sound travels around the hall is critical, so good design is very important. In modern buildings, the acoustics are often tested with scale models of the hall. A good concert hall does not try to eliminate all echoes (reflected sounds), as this would make the sound in the hall seem very flat and lifeless. Echoes actually make the sounds richer, so a concert hall needs to make good use of them. The concert hall also needs to be designed so that everybody in the audience can hear well. Reverberation is an important factor in listening pleasure. It occurs when the sound can still be heard fading away for several seconds after the music has actually stopped being produced. Most concert halls are designed for a two-second reverberation time, but in a large cathedral, this time can be as long as eight seconds. The longer reverberation time produces a very different sound.

Designers avoid using too much padded furniture, carpets and wall hangings in a concert hall, as these surfaces, absorb sound. They also avoid too many hard or flat surfaces which can increase the reverberation time. Instead, they prefer to use suspended ceilings and angled boxes that reflect the sound toward the audience.

Modern concert halls use baffles (sound reflectors) suspended from the ceiling of the hall to improve the acoustics.

EXPERIMENT

Ripple tanks

If you drop a stone into a pond the ripples will spread out in circles (see page 8). The speed at which the ripples will travel depends on the depth of water. If the ripples are bounced off a curved surface, they will travel in straight lines. Many concert halls have a curved wall both behind the audience and behind the stage. This helps to deflect the sound waves toward the audience.

In this experiment you will use a shallow container to act as a ripple tank. You will need a large and deep baking tray or similar shaped container, some ink, an eye dropper, a flexible strip of metal or plastic (such as a long ruler) and a stopwatch.

1 Fill the container with 10–15 mm (about ½ in.) of water. Raise one end of the container to a height of approximately 1 cm (½ in.) and then gently drop it. Watch the ripples move across the container. Use the stopwatch to measure the time it takes for a ripple to reach the other end. You may need to repeat this several times to get an average reading.
2 Repeat the experiment, but add more water to the tray so that the water is 20 mm (about 1 in.) deep. What effect does the depth of water have on the speed at which the ripples travel?

3 Fill the dropper with some ink. Carefully drop the ink into the middle of the tray. Watch how the ripples spread out across the tray. The ink should help you see clearly what is happening.
4 Refill the tray with fresh water. Position the plastic strip inside the container so that it forms a curved "back wall" (see photograph). Fill the eye dropper with some more ink and drop the ink into the center of the tray as before. How does the curved wall affect the movement of the ripples?

Noise

Whales suffer from noise pollution. A global research project due to last several years is using sound channels in the oceans (see page 24) to transmit high-power noise signals. These are interfering with whale communication.

There are many different sounds in the world, some pleasant and others less attractive. Noise is sound that is unpleasant and which you do not usually want to hear. A musical sound is more pleasing to the ear because the sound consists of a fundamental note and several harmonics (see page 26) and the sound has a regular waveform. Noise, on the other hand, has an irregular pattern of sound waves made up of unrelated frequencies. The source of "noisy" sounds is often very varied, as they are usually caused by irregular sound waves resulting from friction (the rubbing of two surfaces together) and impact. A totally random combination of sounds is known as "white noise."

People do not always agree on what is "noise" and what is "sound." Some people think that modern rock music, for example, is only noise because they do not recognize the waveforms of the music. Someone who likes and listens to a lot of rock music can

Trees are often planted beside major roads to help reduce the noise generated by the traffic.

! *Some personal stereos can produce sounds that exceed 120 dB at the outside of the ear. A similar noise level would be unacceptable in a factory if it lasted for more than 15 seconds!*

recognize the sound patterns it contains. The same disagreement may occur when people listen to music from a different culture.

Noise is very often generated by machinery and can be irritating or dangerous. It can even be considered as a form of environmental pollution. Road traffic is a very common source of noise, generated mostly by the sound of contact between tires and road surface, by air being pushed aside and by engine noise.

Living screens of trees can be an effective sound barrier. Trees are usually planted along highways and other main roads in an attempt to reduce the sound traveling away from the road. The leaves of the trees reflect and absorb the sound in a similar way to human-made soundproofing materials.

Soundproofing

! *In some special soundproofed rooms, called anechoic chambers, the walls absorb 99 percent of the sound energy striking them. It is so quiet in an anechoic chamber that you can hear the food churning in your stomach and the blood pumping through your veins.*

Soundproofing is the process of reducing noise. Random and irregular noise can be reduced, and sometimes even totally eradicated, by a number of different techniques. One basic method of sound reduction is to absorb vibrations, since anything that can vibrate will carry sound. This is rather like damping vibration in buildings and cars (see page 13). Sound travels best through a solid or liquid, and much less well through air (see page 7). Objects that are springy and contain lots of air holes do not conduct sound as well as solid objects. Foam rubber and similar light, airy materials are therefore ideal for soundproofing. Sheets of these materials are placed around the source of the noise, preventing it from escaping by absorbing the sound energy. People working in noisy places such as airports, roadworks or rifle ranges have to wear ear protectors to protect their ears from too much noise. These ear protectors often consist of foam-lined shells that deaden

Airport ground staff wear ear protectors (left) to muffle the sounds of the airplane engines.

Scientists often use an anechoic chamber (above) to test pieces of equipment.

What are the most common sources of noise in your home or school? How could the noise be reduced?

Key Words
Acoustics the behavior of sound in a particular room or space, such as a concert hall or recording studio.
Noise an irregular pattern of sound waves consisting of unrelated frequencies.
Reverberation the echo of a sound played several seconds earlier.
Soundproofing an artificial reduction in the transmission of sound.

the sounds. Sometimes they are specially designed to absorb only certain frequencies of sound, so that speech, for example, can still be heard. Sounds within a building can be reduced by laying thick carpets and putting up heavy curtains and soft wall coverings. Padded furniture can also reduce unwanted noise.

Soundproofing tiles, also called acoustic tiles, work on a similar principle. They too contain air spaces to absorb the energy. They are also specially shaped so that sound energy is not reflected back into the room. This makes them particularly well suited to use in recording studios, where the sound of musical instruments would be distorted if there were strong echoes from the walls.

Double glazing is quite an efficient way of reducing sound, since the two panes of glass are separated by air. However, the air gap in most double glazing is designed to reduce heat loss. A much wider air gap is better for sound insulation. This is why many airport hotels, which suffer particularly high noise levels, use triple glazed panels with two air gaps. One gap is best for heat retention, while the other is designed for noise reduction.

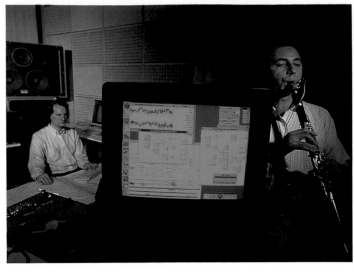

Sounds produced in a recording studio are first checked to ensure the signal is strong enough and then recorded.

Recording and reproducing sound

We know that sounds are simply a series of pressure waves, causing changes in the pressure of the air (see pages 6–7). So, if the changing pressure of the air can be accurately recorded, the sound may be reproduced later. Until relatively recently, sound recording has been an analog process throughout. The term *analog* means that information concerning the frequency and amplitude of the sound waves is represented by a continuous electrical signal. However, more and more elements of the recording and playback process now make use of digital techniques to improve the quality of sound reproduction. To understand the difference between analog and digital, it is helpful to think of analog and digital watches. An analog watch has two hands: the position of these hands indicates the time, as they move around the clock's face smoothly and continously. A digital watch, by contrast, uses numbers to show the time directly. Digital watches are much more accurate than their analog counterparts, but they flick from one number to another rather than showing a graduated (bit-by-bit) movement.

Analog recording

A vinyl record has a spiral groove on its surface. To play the music a stylus or needle is dragged along the groove as the record spins on the turntable. (Below: a highly magnified view of a stylus in a groove.)

In analog recording, the sound waves are collected by a microphone (see page 17) and sent to the recorder as a continuously varying electrical voltage. In a tape recorder, this varying voltage is used to vary the level of magnetization of a magnetic tape. This is achieved by using special recording heads that generate a magnetic field. This field magnetizes metal particles on the surface of the tape. As the tape is passed over the recording head, the strength of the magnetic field changes in proportion to the signals from the microphone. The tape stores a "magnetic history" of these changes along its length. When the music is to be played back, a playback head capable of measuring magnetic field strength is used to measure the magnetism of the tape. It is very important that the recording and playback tape speeds are the same. The playback head produces changes in the voltage, which is almost the same as that recorded by the microphone. This voltage is amplified and sent to a loudspeaker, and the sound is reproduced.

Digital recording

Digital recording uses a rather different method. The continuous electric signals from the microphone are sampled very rapidly by an electronic circuit known as an Analog to Digital Converter (ADC). The original signal voltage is converted by the ADC into a stream of numbers, each of which represents the voltage amplitude at a certain point in time. These numbers are in binary format (a sequence of 1s and 0s). When compact discs, usually called CDs, are made, the binary digits are etched by a laser into pits in the disc's surface. This stores the sound on the CD. When the sound is played back, a less powerful laser illuminates the spinning disc and the reflections from the pits in the surface are detected, regenerating the recorded sequence of 0s and 1s. Another electrical circuit, a Digital to Analog Converter (DAC), is the opposite in function to an ADC. It is used to change the digital data back into analog format – that is, into a continuously varying voltage. During the recording process, the sampling of the wave form by the ADC is carried out at very short intervals or high frequency (44,100 times per second), as digital circuits would need infinite storage to handle continuously changing signals. Because digital circuits can work quickly, if the source is sampled rapidly enough the human ear cannot detect that the reconstituted waveform is very slightly different from the original. The limit of human hearing is 20 kHz (kiloHertz), whereas CDs can reproduce sound to 22 kHz. The sampling rate (that is, the rate at which the ADC measures the voltage and converts it into binary data) has to be theoretically twice that of the highest frequency sound to be recorded for acceptable results. This means that, to record music that contains frequencies of 20,000 Hz, a sampling rate of 40,000 Hz is required throughout. The use of a digital re-coding and playback process reduces unwanted noise.

The latest personal CDs (called Minidiscs) can now record music at near perfect quality. They can store up to 74 minutes of music on a disc only 5.0 cm (2 in.) in diameter using a technique called Bit Rate Reduction. This reduces the amount of digital data required to replay the audio. The photograph shows a Minidisc player.

Key Words

Analog information in the form of continous physical quantities such as electrical current and decibels.

Digital information in the form of binary numbers or digits.

Sample to test or measure something.

Voltage a unit of measure of electrical potential (it can be thought of as electrical pressure).

Ultrasound and infrasound

Sounds at frequencies above the range of human hearing are known as ultrasound. Such sounds are in the range of 20,000 to 100,000 Hz or more. Ultrasound does not travel far because the wavelengths are extremely short and carry little energy, so they are quickly absorbed by walls and carpets. Many small animals make use of ultrasound for just this reason – the sound waves they emit do not travel far, so they are less likely to be heard by predators. For example, mice can live under floorboards and safely "chatter" among themselves without cats hearing them.

Echolocation

One effective way of discovering the position of an object is to send out a signal and catch the echo of the sound wave that bounces off and comes back from the object. The time interval between sending the signal and receiving the echo is measured, so that the distance of the object can be calculated.

An echo can be produced in the mountains, in a street or even in a very large building. In fact it can be produced anywhere there is a surface that will reflect sound waves. You can clap your hands and count the seconds that elapse until you hear the echo. Since sound travels at about 340 m/s in air, you can multiply the number of seconds by 340 and divide by two (because the sound has traveled out and back). The resulting figure will give you the distance to the cliff or wall from which the echo came. This process is known as echo-location. It has useful applications in both the natural and human-made worlds.

Bats are nocturnal mammals. Since they fly at night they cannot use sight. As a result many bats, especially the insect-eating variety, have developed echolocation to enable them to find their prey. They emit ultrasonic pulses of sound and use the echoes from these pulses as a natural echo locator. A special instrument can convert the pulses of ultrasound into sounds that we are able to hear. The bats emit a series of clicks, each lasting

People often make use of echoes to communicate between valleys in mountainous areas.

Echolocation enables many bats to detect and catch their prey at night.

Some tiger moths are able to jam the ultrasonic emissions of bats.

! *Some bats produce ultrasonic sounds at such a high frequency that they can detect the presence of a wire no thicker than a human hair placed across their path.*

about 10–20 ms, at a rate of 5 or more clicks per second. They radiate or project a narrow beam of sound in front of them. They have two large ears to recapture the reflected sound. When a bat approaches an interesting object, the frequency of its clicks increases to 200 per second, while the duration of an individual click is reduced to about 1 ms. High frequency sounds are much better for directional precision than lower frequencies, for they carry less energy and spread less widely into the air. Very high frequency sounds are therefore more useful for pinpointing small objects. Furthermore, in order to reflect sound waves an object must be above a certain size relative to the wavelength. So the shorter the wavelength, the smaller the object that can be detected. The little brown bat can use ultrasound with frequencies of 100,000 Hz and find objects as small as 0.3 mm (.012 in.) in diameter.

By emitting louder sounds, a bat is able to detect objects further away. In fact many bats produce sounds that would be the equivalent of a pneumatic drill if we could hear them. However, such loud sounds would overload the bat's very sensitive ears, so it has a muscle in the middle ear that is connected to the hammer bone (see page 15). As a click is made by the bat, this muscle pulls the hammer momentarily out of position, so that it is no longer in contact with the eardrum and the sound is not heard. The muscle then relaxes so that the hammer bone is in position to hear the echo. The echo will not be as loud as the original sound, so can be heard safely by the bat.

Some insects can detect a bat's ultrasonic beams and take evasive action. These insects respond by immediately closing their wings and falling out of the sky in an attempt to avoid the bat. Some tiger moths are even able to jam the bat's sonar by producing their own ultrasound to confuse the bat. Scientists now believe that some moths emit ultrasound as a warning to predators that they are unpleasant to eat.

Some bats can also work out the speed and direction in which their prey is traveling by measuring the changes in the frequency of the echo's sound waves. These bats use the Doppler effect (see page 10) to help them locate and track their prey.

EXPERIMENT

Timing echoes

In this experiment you will work out the speed of sound using echoes bouncing off a wall. You will need a stopwatch, a hammer and a block of hard wood.

1 Find a large brick or concrete wall. Stand as far away from the wall as possible, ideally at least 50 m (165 ft.) away.

2 Try out the method by banging on the wooden block once and listening for the echo. It is very difficult to time the return of a single echo accurately, so it is better to measure the time for 10 or more echoes. You will need to time your bangs so that you hit the wood just as you hear the echo from the previous bang. You may need to practice this a few times. If you feel that 10 times is still too quick you can try 20 bangs.

3 Start the stopwatch as you bang the wood block for the first time and stop it after the tenth and final echo returns. Divide the time elapsed by 10 to find the time for a single echo. If you carried out 20 bangs divide the time by 20 and so on.

4 In order to calculate the speed of sound, you need to work out the distance to the wall and back. Then you divide the distance by the time taken for one echo to return. For example if the distance to the wall and back was 100 m (330 ft.) and the time for one echo was 0.35 seconds, then you would divide 100 by 0.35. Compare your answer to the speed of sound in air, 340 m/s. How close was your answer? Can you think of any ways to improve the design of this experiment?

Sonar

A ship using sonar

Human-made echo locators on ships allow the crew to calculate how deep the sea is or whether there is an object in the water, such as a shoal of fish or a wreck. A piece of equipment called a transducer is used to produce the sound waves. The transducer is a kind of combined underwater loudspeaker and microphone (see page 17), since it converts electrical pulses into pressure waves that it directs toward the seabed. Echoes returning to the transducer are changed back into electrical signals of varying strength and displayed on a video monitor. The echo locator can detect solid matter on the sea floor and hence show the depth of water under the ship's keel. SONAR stands for Sound Navigation And Ranging. It is similar to echolocation but uses a transducer, or a series of transducers, that provide directional information. It is more precise in locating objects under water as it emits one or more narrow, cone-shaped beams of sound. There are two types of sonar, called active and passive sonar. Both are commonly used by naval ships for detecting submarines or surface ships. Active sonar emits a stream of high frequency pulses that are reflected from the

A dolphin's sonar is so sensitive that it can even detect flatfish lying beneath a layer of sand on the seabed.

Both dolphins (right) and naval ships (opposite, below) make use of sonar to detect underwater objects such as shoals of fish or submarines.

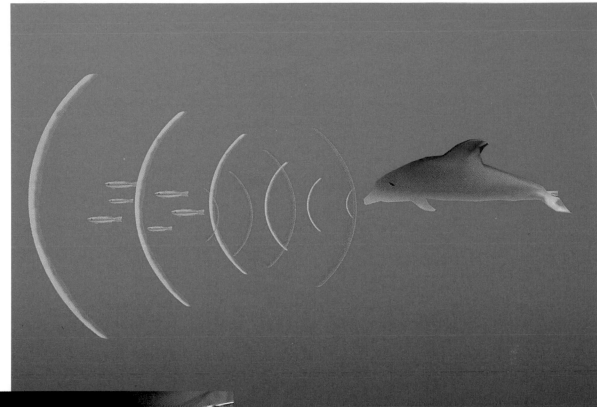

Cave swiftlets use active sonar to navigate around the huge, dark caves of Southeast Asia in which they nest.

Zoologists swimming with killer whales have actually felt the whales "pinging" their bodies with their sonar as the whales tried to distinguish the zoologists from their prey, the seal!

hull of a target, such as a submarine. The measurement of the angle of arrival of the echo, the time it takes to return and any Doppler shift (see page 10) enables the ship's command and control center to plot the target's position, course and speed. However, active sonar signals can be detected by the submarine, so if the ship's captain wishes to keep his own position secret, he will probably use passive sonar. This technique uses microphones only (see page 17) to listen for the noise generated by machinery to locate and identify a target. Often the microphones are towed behind the ship in a cable hundreds of meters long, in order to get away from the ship's own noise. Sonar operators listen to the same frequency bands that are used for communication by whales (see pages 23–24), so they have to become skilled in distinguishing them from ships. The range of a typical sonar system is up to about 4,000 to 6,000 m (13,200 to 19,800 ft.).

A form of active sonar is well developed in the natural world. Whales, dolphins, shrews and some birds, such as the cave swiftlet, make use of it. The whale and dolphin use sonar to locate objects in murky waters. This helps them avoid colliding with underwater obstructions or other animals, and hunt their food. Dolphins are able to produce sonar clicks by forcing air through special passages and sinuses in its head. These clicks are focused into a beam by an oval shaped, fatty organ called the melon. This organ forms the characteristic bulge on the dolphin's forehead.

Ultrasound and medicine

Why is it better for a doctor to treat kidney stones with ultrasound rather than perform an operation?

Ultrasound has many uses for humans, especially in medicine. A common modern use of ultrasound is found in hospitals, where it produces images of unborn babies in the uterus. The unborn baby is scanned with a very narrow beam of very high frequency ultrasound. The sound is produced by a crystal within the scanner that vibrates extremely rapidly, generating short pulses of sound that travel right through the mother and baby. An echo is produced when the speed of the sound wave changes, such as when the sound wave passes from one tissue type into another, perhaps from muscle to bone. This echo is detected by a microphone. The echoes are then amplified and displayed on a screen. The angle of the beam is swept back and forth automatically and, as the beam scans backward and forward, an image of the unborn baby is built up on the screen. Although it takes some skill to recognize what the pictures are showing, the images are sufficiently detailed for a doctor to spot any abnormalities. Specialist doctors can even operate on unborn babies, using ultrasound images to guide them.

Pregnant women are scanned with a narrow beam of high frequency ultrasound (between one million and twenty million Hz). It causes no discomfort or damage to the mother or the baby.

More powerful ultrasonic vibrations can be used to break up unwanted solid deposits in the body, such as kidney stones. These stones are very hard and can cause considerable pain. The stones used to be removed by surgery, but today doctors use an ultrasonic gun. The gun emits short bursts of very high frequency vibrations that cause the stones to resonate. The energy the kidney stones receive (see pages 11–12) causes them to fragment into tiny pieces.

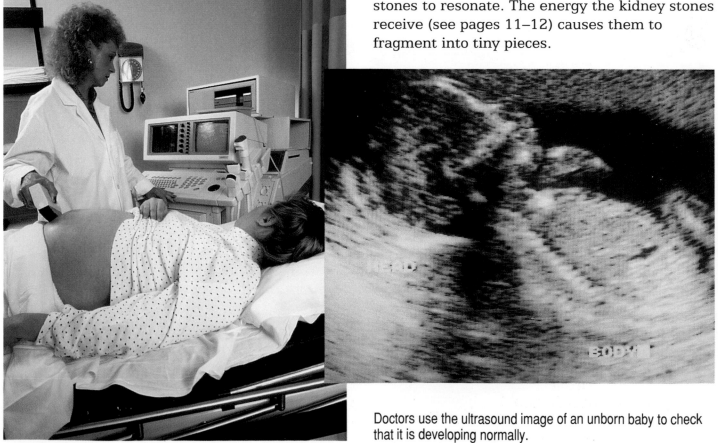

Doctors use the ultrasound image of an unborn baby to check that it is developing normally.

Infrasound

It is thought that migratory birds may build up an infrasound "map" of a route, rather as we would use a road map or visual memories.

Infrasound is the term given to very low frequency sounds that are below the range of human hearing. Some birds can detect sounds as low as 0.1 Hz - just one sound wave every 10 seconds. Scientists now believe that many birds, especially those that migrate over thousands of miles, are able to detect infrasound and use it to help them navigate. For example, swallows, storks and whooper swans may all detect infrasound. Mountains, deserts, oceans and rivers all produce their own characteristic sound patterns that a bird may be able to recognize and identify.

Weather also produces infrasound patterns. For example, an approaching thunderstorm produces not only thunderclaps (see page 9) but also a pattern of infrasound. These patterns can be detected hundreds of miles away from the actual thunderstorm. Some birds, such as the African guinea fowl, seem to be able to predict weather and change their behavior accordingly. These birds usually live in groups, but just before the rains come they split up and establish territories for breeding. Although the rains never arrive on the same day each year, the birds unfailingly establish their territories just a day or so before the rains arrive. It is now believed that they detect the infrasound of approaching rainstorms.

Animals often behave differently just before an earthquake so by observing animal behavior people can be forewarned of an earthquake

African guinea fowl detect changes in the weather by sensing infrasound patterns.

Key words
Echo a reflected sound.
Infrasound sounds of very low frequency, usually between 0.1 and 10 Hz.
Sonar a method of locating objects under water by the reflection of sound waves.
Ultrasound sounds of very high frequency, usually somewhere between 20,000 and 100,000 Hz.

The future

Much of the future of sound technology will concern developments for producing and, more importantly, controlling sound. Many of these techniques are in their infancy, for only in recent years have computers become powerful enough to calculate accurately the behavior of sound waves in a complex three-dimensional space.

Noise cancellation is a particularly important new technology, for it provides the potential of removing unwanted noise. The technique relies upon detecting and then generating a "mirror image" of the noise waveform extremely rapidly. Each sound wave has a trough and peak. If the trough of one wave intersects with a peak of another wave of exactly the same frequency and amplitude, the waves will cancel one another out. The mirror image signal, technically known as "180 degrees out-of-phase," is amplified to the same level as the noise, and the two signals will then cancel one another out, thereby eliminating the noise.

The design of a noise cancellation (or anti-noise) system is quite simple. A sound monitor determines the frequency and loudness of the sound and feeds it into a processor that will produce an exactly opposite (mirror image) signal. The mirror image is amplified and then output through loudspeakers. A microphone continuously checks the performance of the anti-noise unit and makes adjustments where necessary.

Outdoor concerts experience particular problems because sound does not travel well through air (see page 8). Even though amplified, the music loses quality. Orchestral sound tends to be weak and flat outdoors because the high and low frequencies tend to disperse more quickly than sounds in the middle frequency range. The further away a person is from the stage, the less high and low frequencies he or she hears. Furthermore, the reverberation created by sounds bouncing off the walls of a concert hall is also absent, contributing to the degradation (reduction) of sound quality. However, new developments should significantly improve outdoor concerts in the future.

A new signal processing technique is being researched at the NASA Ames Research Center in California. This may soon help to make air travel even safer and has many other possible applications. The

Noise cancellation systems are fitted to the headphones of aircraft pilots to cancel out any noises that cause stress or damage hearing.

technique combines the processing of signals with computers to ensure that sounds appear to come from specific directions and at specific noise levels. This is known as "virtual acoustics." A special headset tells the computer the exact position and direction of the wearer's head. The radio messages from the aircraft seem to the wearer to be coming from different directions and from different distances away.

By reducing unwanted noise and improving the quality of what we do hear, these and other technological advances will increase our enjoyment of the rich variety of sound in the world.

A better understanding of acoustics may mean that outdoor concerts will sound as good as those performed in concert halls.

Air traffic controllers will soon be able to use the technique of virtual acoustics in monitoring aircraft movements.

Glossary

acoustics the behavior of sound in a particular room or space, such as a concert hall.

amplitude the height of the peak of a wave above an imaginary line running along the middle of the waveform.

analog information in the form of continuous physical quantities such as size of electrical current, number of decibels.

diaphragm a thin membrane that can vibrate.

digital information stored as a set of binary numbers or digits.

ear the organ concerned with hearing in animals.

echo a reflected sound.

frequency the number of sound waves that pass a particular point per second.

fundamental the lowest harmonic of a musical tone.

harmonics a series of partial vibrations that combine to form a musical tone.

infrasound sounds of very low frequency, usually between 0.1 and 10 Hz.

larynx the organ that produces sound in mammals.

longitudinal lying long ways.

loudspeaker an electromechanic device that converts electrical signals into sound waves.

microphone a device that converts sound waves into electrical signals.

noise an irregular pattern of sound waves consisting of unrelated frequencies.

octave a set of eight musical notes.

pitch a measure of the frequency of a sound, for example a high frequency sound has a high pitch.

resonance a condition that occurs when an object is vibrated at a frequency matching one of its own natural frequencies.

reverberation the echo of a sound produced several seconds earlier.

sample to test or measure something

sonar a method of locating objects by the reflection of sound waves.

soundproofing an artificial reduction in the transmission of sound.

transducer something that is capable of converting energy from one form to another.

ultrasound sounds of very high frequency, usually between 20,000 and 100,000 Hz.

vibration a back and forth movement, or oscillation.

voltage a unit of measure of electrical potential (it can be thought of as electrical pressure).

wave a disturbance in a medium, such as air in water, that occurs at regular intervals.

wavelength the distance between the peaks or troughs of two adjacent waves.

Answers to the questions

p. 8 Sound waves are produced by particles moving backward and forward in the direction of the wave, whereas waves moving across water are caused by the up-and-down motion of particles at 90° to the direction of the wave.

p. 9 Because light travels faster than sound.

p. 12 So that the vibrations produced are irregular and do not match the natural frequency of the bridge.

p. 20 Low frequency sounds travel better through the forest.

p. 21 Dead trees contain more air spaces. These allow the sound to resonate, acting as a natural amplifier just like the body of a guitar.

p. 25 Musical notes consist of specific frequencies and amplitudes, whereas noise is random in both frequencies and amplitudes.

p. 26 Plucking: guitar, ukelele, lute, sitar, harp, banjo. Hitting: piano, clavichord, dulcimer. Bowing: cello, violin, viola.

p. 28 The hollow shell amplifies certain frequencies of sound. The sounds remind many people of waves crashing on a beach.

p. 29 Tension affects the frequency or pitch of a note as well as its duration. The tighter the skin of the drum, the shorter the wavelength and hence the higher the pitch of the beat and the shorter its duration.

p. 35 Home and school — voices, music being played, radio, television, door slamming. Reduce these by better soundproofing, heavy curtains and wall coverings, soft furnishings, double-glazed windows, preventing people from making the noise, i.e. school rules.

p. 42 Ultrasound is quicker since there is no need to operate. The patient does not have to stay in the hospital. It is cheaper, less painful, and there is less chance of infection and fewer complications.

Index

Key words appear in **boldface** type